Brickwork

Techniques & Projects

MINI · WORKBOOK · SERIES

MEREHURST

CONTENTS

*Reconstituted stone retaining walls and slab paving
(top), a block barbecue (far left) and a brick wall (left)*

Bricks and blocks can be used in a wide variety of different ways in the garden—for walls, for steps and for paving.

Bricks and bricklaying

Strong, attractive brickwork results from a careful choice of bricks and neat, precise bricklaying.

Most bricks used around the home are made from clay or shale fired in a kiln or oven. Calcium silicate bricks are made from sand or crushed flint and hardened under steam pressure whilst concrete bricks (referred to as 'blocks') are made from cement mixed with aggregates.

Bricks are made to a 'modular' size, 225 mm long, 112.5 mm thick and 75 mm high. This module includes one 10 mm mortar course, so that the actual size of the brick is 215 x 102.5 x 65 mm: two module thicknesses or three module heights equal one module length—an important relationship in bricklaying.

Bricks can be cut using a club hammer and bolster chisel. A half brick is known as a bat. The brick or block you choose for a project depends on its type, its variety and its quality. It may also be described by its colour or where it was made.

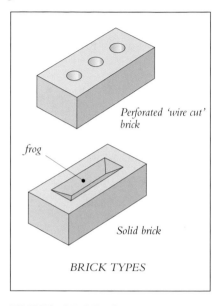

Perforated 'wire cut' brick

frog

Solid brick

BRICK TYPES

To cut bricks hold a bolster steady at the appropriate point and strike it firmly with a club hammer.

TYPES OF BRICK
• Solid bricks are the most familiar and often have a frog (a depression in one face) from the manufacturing process. They can be machine made (moulded or pressed) or hand made.
• Perforated bricks have holes running through the thickness (so vertical when laid). If the holes make up less than 25 per cent of the volume, the brick is classified as solid. Many perforated bricks are known as 'wirecut' as they are cut with a wire after being extruded though a die in the making process.
• Shaped bricks are for corners, sills and cappings (tops of walls).

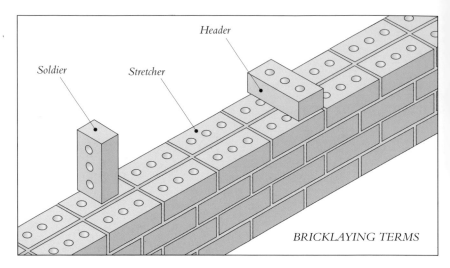

Soldier   *Stretcher*   *Header*

BRICKLAYING TERMS

VARIETIES OF BRICK

The three common varieties of brick are used for different purposes.

- Common bricks are used for general building work, especially for walls which will later be plastered or rendered. Many common bricks are described as flettons.
- Facing bricks are used where they will be seen and have at least one acceptable face. Normally stronger and better quality than common bricks, they are used for garden walls and external house walls.
- Engineering bricks are very dense and are strong and resistant to moisture. This makes them suitable for use in retaining walls and for courses of wall below ground level.

BRICK QUALITIES

This refers to weather resistance.

- Ordinary bricks are suitable for the outside face of a building, but should be frost resistant if used in garden walls.

- Special quality bricks are durable even when soaking wet and are suitable for all garden walling, including retaining walls.
- Internal bricks are only suitable for walls inside the house.

CONCRETE BLOCKS

For garden walling, 'reconstituted stone' blocks are a popular choice. Made mainly from concrete, they give the appearance of natural stone. They come in single units (roughly the same size as a brick) and multiple units, the size of several bricks, with mortar courses already in place.

LAYING BRICKS

Bricks can be laid in different ways. The terms most often used are:

- stretcher—laid lengthwise in a wall;
- header—laid through a wall, at right angles to stretchers;
- soldier—stood on end or on edge (often used on the tops of walls).

TYPES OF BRICKS

Interlocking clay paver

Moulded stock facing brick

Clay paver

Hand-made stock facing brick

Extruded common brick

Sand-faced facing brick

Double bullnose brick for capping

'Reconstituted stone' concrete walling block

Multiple concrete walling block

Pierced screen walling block

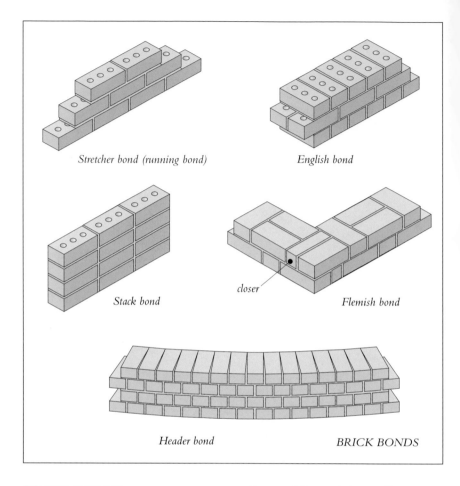

Stretcher bond (running bond)

English bond

Stack bond

closer

Flemish bond

Header bond

BRICK BONDS

BRICK BONDS

For maximum strength, successive layers (courses) of brick are lapped one over the other. This overlapping is known as bonding. Poor bonding can lead to weakness in a wall.

• In stretcher bond (running bond) all the bricks are laid as stretchers. Used for general construction work.

• In English bond, alternate courses of bricks are laid as headers and stretchers. A very strong bond, it is often used for retaining walls.

• In Flemish bond (another strong bond), each course consists of alternate headers and pairs of stretchers. Half-brick 'closers' are needed on each course.

• In stack bond the bricks are laid vertically on top of each other (the bricks must all be exactly the same size). This is a very weak bond and it is used only for feature panels or screen block walls.

- In header bond all the bricks are laid as headers. Most often used for circular walls or curved brickwork.

BRICKLAYING

Accuracy and neatness are very important for bricklaying. Brickwork must be checked frequently for plumb (vertical) and for level.

Keep the work area neat and tidy, free of broken bricks and old mortar, so you don't fall over them or dirty the new brickwork. Store bricks and sand close to the work site, and cover them to keep them dry. Store bags of cement and lime in a dry area.

CALCULATING THE NUMBER OF BRICKS

In order to build 1 sq m of single-thickness brick wall you will need sixty bricks. To calculate how many bricks you will need for a wall, follow these steps:

1 Find the overall area of the wall to be built by multiplying the length by the height in metres.

2 Calculate the areas of any openings and subtract these from the overall area.

3 Multiply the area by 60 to find the number of bricks required for a single-thickness wall.

4 If the wall is to be two bricks thick, then multiply the overall area of the wall by 120.

MATCHING BRICKS AND MORTAR

When bricking up unwanted openings in brick walls or adding a new section of wall, you need to carefully match the existing bricks for size and texture. If the wall is to be left unpainted, you will also need to match the bricks for colour.

In the UK, bricks are now made to a metric format and the main size problem is matching new metric bricks to old imperial ones. The best chance will be to buy second-hand bricks from an architectural salvage yard, where you may also get a good match in texture and colour. If you cannot get matching bricks, increase the size of the mortar courses by 1.2 mm.

It can also be difficult to find the correct mix and colour for the mortar. The following is a rough guide to mortar colours (see also page 21). Experiment with the mix to get a precise match. Remember to let the new mix dry before comparing it with the existing mortar.
- White mortar. Use white sand, white cement and lime.
- Grey mortar. Use a mix of bricklayer's sand (loam colour) and grey cement.
- Red mortar. Use bricklayer's sand, grey cement and red oxide.
- Black mortar. Use bricklayer's sand, grey cement and black oxide.

Preparing the site

Careful setting out is the first step for any successful bricklaying project. You may need to consult a surveyor for large projects or those close to a boundary.

TOOLS AND MATERIALS

- Measuring tape
- Timber stakes
- Timber for profiles
- Nails and hammer
- String
- Spirit level
- Line level
- Plumb bob
- Builder's square
- 12 mm clear tube water level
- Spade

SETTING OUT

Measure out the outline of your job and erect timber profiles about 1 m beyond the outline. This keeps them out of the way when you are digging the foundation trenches. Tie string lines to the nails in the profiles to indicate the width of the trench (see page 13) and walls to act as guides. Then sprinkle a line of lime exactly under the string line to provide a guide for digging.

When setting out trenches, ensure the corners are at right angles. Check with a builder's square or use

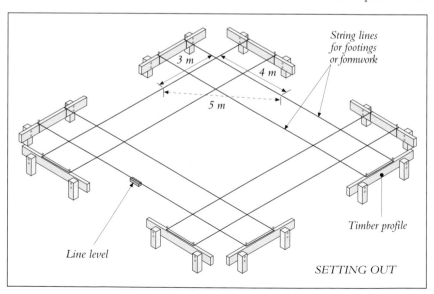

String lines for footings or formwork

3 m

4 m

5 m

Timber profile

Line level

SETTING OUT

Each panel of this high brick wall is stepped down so that the wall maintains an even height down the slope. Because the steps are large, the capping bricks are also stepped to achieve a more flowing effect.

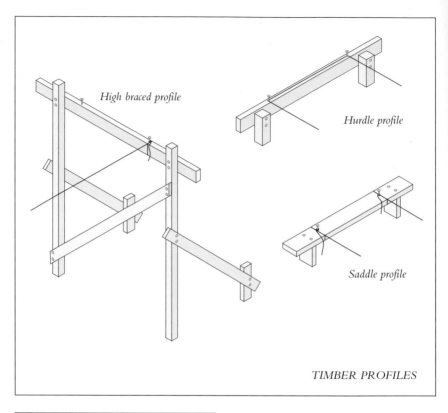

High braced profile

Hurdle profile

Saddle profile

TIMBER PROFILES

the 3-4-5 method (see the diagrams here and on page 10). Measure along one side 3 m from the corner and then 4 m along the other side (or you can use any multiples of these

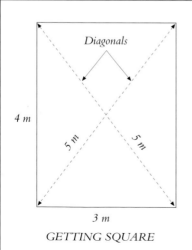

Diagonals

4 m

5 m

5 m

3 m

GETTING SQUARE

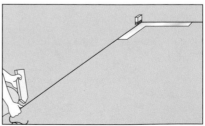

A builder's square can be used to check the corners of the area are square when setting string lines.

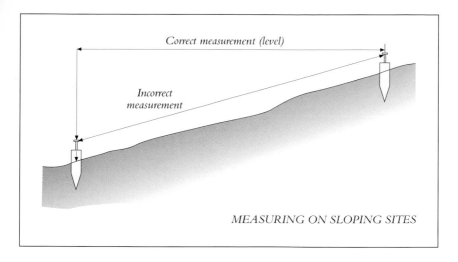

Correct measurement (level)

Incorrect measurement

MEASURING ON SLOPING SITES

numbers, for example, 300 and 400 mm, or 600 and 800 mm). The third side of the triangle should equal 5m (or 500 mm or 1 m, as appropriate) if you have made a right angle.

When set out, check that all corners are square by checking the two diagonals are the same length. Measurements should always be taken on the level, even if you are on a sloping site. Use a spirit level to ensure the tape measure is level.

ESTABLISHING LEVELS

When setting out a project, establish levels accurately. Put a timber stake in the ground at each corner of the job. Mark near the top of one stake and mark the other stakes at the same height, using a 12 mm clear tube water level or a timber straight-edge (100 x 25 mm) and spirit level. Adjust each of the string lines to this level and check with a line level hooked on to each string in turn.

FOUNDATION TRENCHES

A single-thickness brick wall up to 750 mm (30 in) high needs concrete foundations (footings) as least 350 mm (14 in) wide and 150 mm (6 in) deep; for double-thickness walls (up to 1.5 m high), use a width of 530 mm (21 in). On sites exposed to wind, increase the width by 50 mm (2 in); on soft (such as clay) soils, increase the depth by 75 mm (3 in).

To find the level for the top of the footings (which should be 150 or 225 mm below ground level), measure down an equal distance from the level mark on each stake. If the ground is not level you may have to step the footings. To make bricklaying easier, each step should be 75 or 150 mm (the height of one or two bricks plus mortar) so that you don't have to cut the bricks.

When digging, keep within the string lines. Keep the sides of the trench vertical and straight.

Concrete footings

Concrete footings are necessary to provide a firm base for a brick wall. Concrete can be mixed by hand, prepared using a concrete mixer or delivered to the site ready mixed.

TOOLS AND MATERIALS

- Timber for formwork
- Timber stakes, nails and hammer
- Steel reinforcement (mesh or bars, stirrups and bar chairs)
- Tie-wire and pliers
- Cement, sand and coarse aggregate
- Concrete mixer (hired)
- Wheelbarrow, shovel and gum boots
- Straight-edge and spirit level
- Steel and wooden floats

FORMWORK

Usually concrete is poured directly into the foundation trench but you may need to build formwork if the footing will rise above ground level.

Formwork is a temporary frame, usually made of timber or plywood, that holds concrete to the required shape until it has hardened. It must be well staked to withstand the pressure of the wet concrete.

Use long pieces of timber and hold them in place with stakes. Use a spirit level to check that the formwork is level.

SIZE OF TRENCHES

Footings are usually twice the width of the finished wall. If you are using formwork, allow 100 mm extra width for the frame and supporting stakes.

STEEL REINFORCEMENT

To give concrete strength and rigidity and prevent it bending under load, it can be reinforced with two layers of steel bars or trench mesh. The bars are tied to stirrups with wire and should overlap a minimum of 450 mm when they join. Place

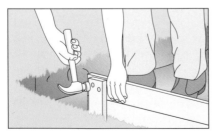

Use stakes to support the formwork and hold it in place. It must withstand the pressure of the concrete.

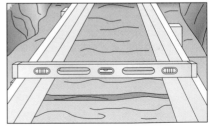

Use a level to check that the formwork is level. You will then be able to level off the concrete easily.

Concrete footings can be reinforced with steel bars or mesh. To hold them in position near the top and bottom of the concrete they are secured to stirrups, which can be suspended by wire from timber beams.

them as near the top and bottom of the concrete as possible (see page 16) and at least 60 mm from the edges. The stirrups can be supported on 'bar chairs' or hung with wire from a beam. The bar chairs are placed at a maximum distance of 600 mm apart.

THE CONCRETE MIX

A mix suitable for wall footings uses cement, concreting ('sharp') sand, coarse (20 mm) aggregate and clean water. The proportions (by volume) should be one part cement, two and a half parts sand and three and a half

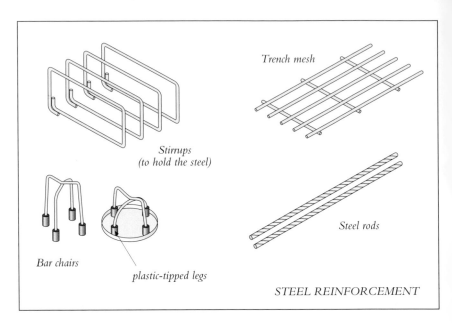

Stirrups
(to hold the steel)

Trench mesh

Bar chairs

plastic-tipped legs

Steel rods

STEEL REINFORCEMENT

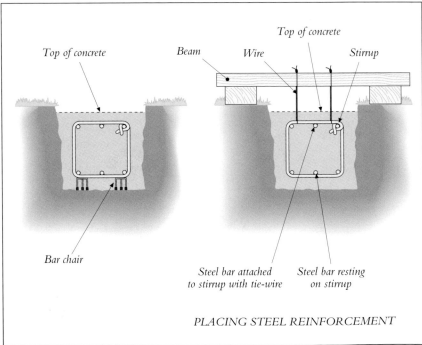

Top of concrete

Beam   Wire

Top of concrete

Stirrup

Top of concrete

Bar chair

Steel bar attached
to stirrup with tie-wire

Steel bar resting
on stirrup

PLACING STEEL REINFORCEMENT

ORDERING FOR CONCRETE

MATERIAL	PROPORTION	QUANTITY TO FILL 1 CU M
Cement	1	5.6 bags
Sand	2½	620 kg
20 mm aggregate	3½	1165 kg

parts 20 mm aggregate (1:2½:3½), and enough water to get it to a workable state. (See table above for quantities.) The concrete should hold its shape without slumping (too wet) or crumbling (too dry).

MIXING BY HAND
Concrete can be mixed by hand using a shovel, especially if only small quantities are required. Prepare the mix in a metal wheelbarrow that can be easily cleaned or on a flat surface that can be hosed down.

1 Mix the cement, sand and coarse aggregate together thoroughly while they are still dry.

2 If you are working on a flat surface, make a well in the centre of the dry mix. Add water and combine until the mix is an even colour and texture.

USING A CONCRETE MIXER
You can also mix concrete in a concrete mixer (they are available for hire). Make sure the mixer is level and on a stable surface.

1 Start by measuring out the amounts of cement, sand and 20 mm

aggregate needed. Note that the proportions are by volume. A typical hired concrete mixer produces around 85 litres of concrete— enough to lay around 1.6 m of footing for a single-thickness wall (1 m for double thickness).

2 Add half the aggregate for one mix to the drum plus some water and, with the drum revolving, add half the cement and sand in small batches.

3 Add the remaining sand, cement and aggregate (with more water as necessary) and continue to mix until the concrete is falling cleanly off the blades. Tip into a wheelbarrow. Clean the mixer immediately—or leave it running with just aggregate and water for the next batch.

READY-MIXED CONCRETE
For large amounts of concrete (for example for the base of a driveway), you can order ready-mixed concrete to be delivered by a truck. Check with local suppliers what their minimum orders are and specify what the concrete is to be used for. Make sure it has a high workability, which give you longer to work with it before it sets hard. Finally, ensure

you have several wheelbarrows available and workers to carry and spread the concrete.

LAYING THE FOOTINGS

Prepare any formwork the day before and start work early in the morning so the concrete will have time to set and can be finished before dark. Step the footings if necessary (see the diagram below). Have all the equipment ready—wheelbarrows, shovels, gum boots, timber lengths to level the concrete as you go, and floats to finish it.

1 Start at the lowest point on the site when laying the concrete, using a shovel or spade to spread it within the formwork. Keep the concrete level, checking it regularly. Make sure the concrete is packed under any steel reinforcement so it doesn't drop. If the stirrups are suspended with tie-wire from a beam, cut the tie-wire with the shovel as you work.

2 Finish the concrete 150 or 225 mm below ground level. (It is difficult to finish it precisely level and if you need to cut bricks in the lowest course they will not then be visible.) Level the concrete roughly with a shovel and then use a wooden or steel float to provide a smooth finish. A steel float gives a smoother finish than a wooden one.

3 The concrete footings must be left to cure for at least two days before you start laying the brickwork or the concrete may crack.

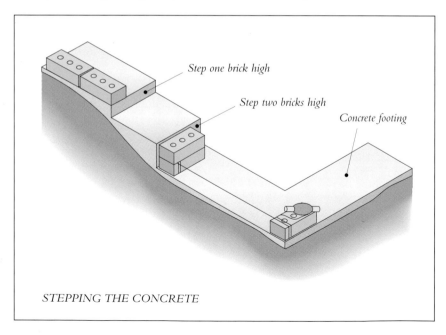

Step one brick high

Step two bricks high

Concrete footing

STEPPING THE CONCRETE

BRICK DRIVEWAYS

Driveways of brick or clay pavers are laid in essentially the same way as other brick paving (see pages 52–5) but because they will have to bear the weight of cars and other vehicles, they need a substantial base.

Most driveways can be laid with a base of 100 mm of compacted hardcore and 50 mm of bedding sand laid as described on pages 58–9, but the hardcore must be well compacted.

For a heavy duty driveway use a base of 100 mm of foundation concrete—a mix of one part cement, two and a half parts sand and three and a half parts 20 mm aggregate $(1:2^1/2:3^1/2)$. When it has set, cover it with 50 mm of sand and then lay the pavers.

Edge restraints concreted in place (see page 55) are essential for any driveway, or the weight of the vehicles will push out the pavers around the edge.

Hardcore and sand are an adequate base for most paved driveways.

Mortars and joints

The secret of laying bricks lies in keeping the mortar at the right consistency. The mortar joints are an integral part of a brick wall, holding the bricks in place and levelling the courses when the bricks are uneven sizes.

TOOLS AND MATERIALS

- Sand, cement and lime, or pre-mixed mortar
- Plasticiser and oxides (optional)
- Plywood mortar board or concrete mixer for mixing mortar
- Shovel
- Measure for oxides (optional)
- Trowel
- Jointer or raking tool

CONSISTENCY

Most amateur bricklayers use mortar that is too dry. To lay bricks you need mortar that is soft and pliable, a bit like toothpaste. Mortar that is too hard is very difficult to spread and joints will be uneven. It is likely to fall off the brick in a lump. Mortar that is too wet will run all over the face of the brickwork.

Mortar is useful for only about one and a half hours (a little water can be added to keep it soft and workable). After that time it loses plasticity and should be thrown out.

MATERIALS

Mortar is made from sand, cement, lime and water.

- Sand is the main ingredient in

mortar, and the best sand to use is bricklayer's sand, also known as soft sand. This is finer than the 'sharp' sand used for making concrete.

- Portland or masonry cement is used for bricklaying. Cement should always be kept dry. If wet it becomes lumpy or goes hard and is unusable. Store it in a garage or shed.
- Hydrated lime (or a plasticiser) is used with Portland cement mortar to make it more workable and retard its setting time. It is purchased in bags and should also be kept dry.
- Always use clean and fresh water.

Mortars made with masonry cement or Portland cement with plasticiser are more resistant to frost damage during construction, whilst cement:lime mortars ('gauged' mortars) are more adhesive and more resistant to water penetration.

MORTAR MIXES

For normal bricklaying, use a mortar mix of one part Portland cement, one part lime and six parts sand (1:1:6) or one part masonry cement to five parts sand (1:5) with all parts by volume. Sills, copings, retaining walls and garden walls exposed to wind need stronger mixes (1:$1/4$:4

Dry pressed bricks in the sandstock range are combined here with off-white mortar to achieve a traditional look. The joints are raked for a neat finish.

with Portland cement or 1:3 for masonry cement). See page 22 for details. For small quantities, use dry ready-mixed bricklaying mortar, sold in bags, to which you add water.

ORDERING MATERIALS FOR MORTAR

The amounts of each material you need depend on the mortar mix. For normal bricklaying, using a 1:1:6 (cement:lime:sand) mix, a 50 kg bag of Portland cement plus 50 kg lime and 330 kg of sand will be enough to lay around 500 bricks. For dry ready-mixed mortar, a 40 kg bag should lay 50 bricks.

MORTAR COLOURS

Oxides can be used to colour mortars. They come in basic colours: yellow, brown, red and black. The amount of oxide added depends on the depth of colour required. Always use a measuring gauge (a jam jar or bottle with the required level marked on it) so the colour remains the same from batch to batch. To check the colour, place the mortar on the back of a brick and leave it in the sun to dry.

For details on achieving specific colours, see the box on page 9.

MORTAR BOARDS

When the mortar has been mixed, transfer it to a mortar board, which makes it easier to pick up the mortar with a trowel.

Mortar boards are usually about 1 sq m and are made from a sheet of waterproof plywood.

MORTAR MIXES (PROPORTIONS BY VOLUME)

PURPOSE	CEMENT	LIME	SAND
Normal (Portland cement)	1	1	6
Normal (masonry cement)	1	–	5
Strong (Portland cement)	1	¼	4
Strong (Portland cement)	1	–	3

WORKING THE MORTAR

To ensure the mortar is soft and pliable, work it continuously on the board, using the trowel or, if it gets really hard, a shovel. Ideally, an assistant makes it while you lay bricks.

1 Use a smooth movement to lift the mortar off the board with a trowel.

2 Throw the mortar back on to the board and then move it to the left, softening it with the tip and edge of the trowel, and then work it back to the right in the same way.

3 Using the back of the trowel, move the mortar back across the board to finish the mixing.

MORTAR JOINTS

The mortar joints between bricks need to be finished off (pointed) whilst the mortar is still workable. There are various joint profiles.

• Flush joint. Suitable for rustic bricks or to give a smooth even surface. Create by removing the excess mortar with a trowel and rubbing the dry joint with sacking.

• Round ironed joint. Also known as a concave or 'bucket handle' joint, this is particularly suitable for use with second-hand bricks. It is created by running a round iron jointer (or a length of tubing) along the joint.

• Raked joint. Made by raking out the mortar with a piece of metal or wood (or a special tool). This joint

1 Lift the mortar off the mortar board with the trowel, using a wrist, elbow and shoulder movement.

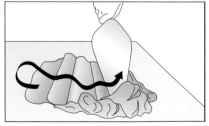

2 Begin softening the mortar by moving it to the left, using the tip and edge of the trowel.

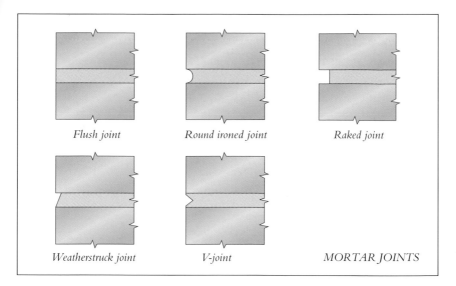

Flush joint   Round ironed joint   Raked joint

Weatherstruck joint   V-joint   *MORTAR JOINTS*

does not shed water so should only be used inside or outside with special quality bricks.

• Weatherstruck joints. Very popular for use on houses, this joint is created by shaping the mortar with a pointing trowel. It sheds water well to help rain run off the brickwork.

• V-joint. Made with a shaped jointing tool, this attractive joint also sheds water well.

Mortar that matches the colour of the bricks gives a modern effect.

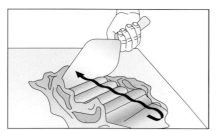

2 Using the same movement, work the mortar back towards the right, thus improving the even consistency.

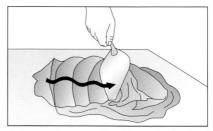

3 Turn the trowel and use the back of it to move the mortar across the board to finish the thorough mixing.

Laying bricks

Trowelling techniques and the methods used to build up a wall are the basic skills needed for bricklaying.

SETTING OUT THE BRICKWORK

Before you start laying bricks, set out the first course of bricks in a dry run to make sure the bonding in the wall is correct. Don't use mortar but allow for 10 mm vertical joints. Work from one corner only so that

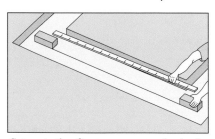

Set out the first course to check the bonding and establish the corners, or use a gauging stick as here.

you don't end up with incorrect bonding in the centre of the wall. When building a structure such as a raised bed, set out two complete sides from a corner (the other two sides will be the same).

It is worth making a gauging stick—a length of timber marked with brick lengths and widths on one side and brick thicknesses on the other (all including mortar joints), so that you can work out how many bricks will be needed along the wall and also to check course heights.

TROWELLING TECHNIQUES

1 Mix up a batch of mortar, place some on the mortar board and work it to a pliable consistency (see the steps illustrated on pages 22–3). Move the mortar to the rear right-hand corner of the board (the rear left-hand corner for left handers).

2 Pick up the trowel but do not grip it too tightly. Work some mortar into the shape of the trowel and lift it off the board by sliding the trowel under it. Pick up only enough mortar to lay two or three bricks.

3 Spread the mortar on the bricks already laid (or the foundations for the first course). It takes practice to

Keeping the courses level and the walls vertical as you build are essential elements in bricklaying. String lines, held in place with corner blocks, help to keep the courses level.

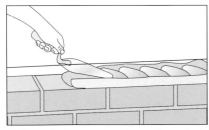

3 Spread the mortar to make a bed, holding the trowel parallel to the wall and forming a series of ridges.

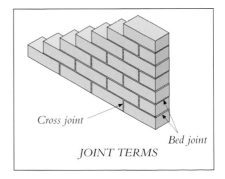

Cross joint

Bed joint

JOINT TERMS

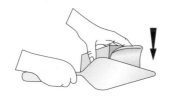

1 Scrape mortar on to end of brick.

2 Spread firmly over end.

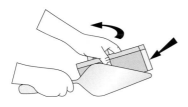

3 Remove excess mortar.

BUTTERING A BRICK TO
PUT ON A CROSS JOINT

LEVEL AND PLUMB

A spirit level is an essential tool for the bricklayer and is used to check that each course is level. It can also be used to check for plumb (vertical) and alignment, but any straight piece of timber can be used for this. If bricks are out of alignment, use your trowel handle to tap them back into place before the mortar dries.

develop the technique of ridging the mortar with the trowel but if the mortar is workable it will be easier. Hold the trowel parallel to the wall when spreading the mortar bed and move it along the wall at the same time. Spread the mortar at an even thickness of about 15–20 mm.

4 To make a cross joint, hold the brick in one hand with the end pointing forwards. Pick up enough mortar with the trowel to cover ('butter') the end of the brick with mortar, spreading it firmly over the end and removing any excess (see the drawings on the left).

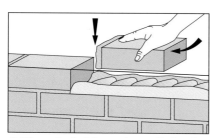

5 Place the brick on the wall, butting it first against the last brick and then pressing down on to the bed.

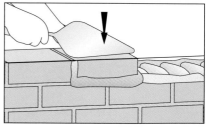

6 Use the trowel to tap the brick into place so that it aligns perfectly. Keep the bed joint an even thickness.

Bed and cross joints of consistent thickness make for neat brickwork.

5 Place the brick on the wall, butting it firmly against the last brick laid and then pressing it down on the laid bed of mortar.

6 Use the trowel to tap the brick into place so that it aligns perfectly and the bed joint is a consistent thickness of about 10 mm.

7 Remove the excess mortar from the bed joint by sliding the trowel along the joint, moving it upwards.

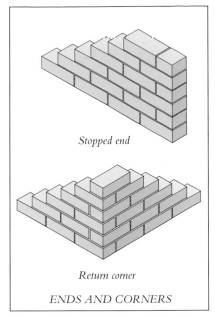

Stopped end

Return corner

ENDS AND CORNERS

8 Bring the trowel back along the bed joint and then up the cross joint to remove excess mortar.

BUILDING UP THE BRICKWORK

1 Start at the ends and corners and work inwards. Lay enough mortar on the foundations for three bricks at an end or three bricks each way at a

7 Slide the trowel along the bed joint to remove the excess mortar and give a neat finish.

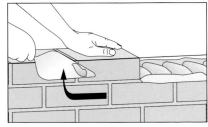

8 Bring the trowel back along the bed joint and then up the cross joint to remove excess mortar.

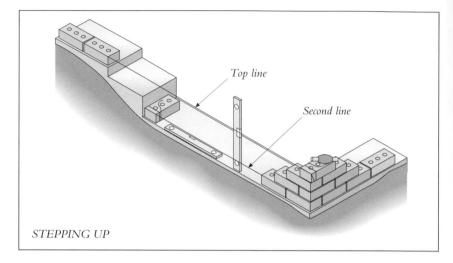

STEPPING UP

corner. Lay these bricks, check that they are level and then build up the end or corner by five courses. Follow the 'Trowelling techniques' (described on pages 25–7), checking the brick course heights with a gauging stick. Ensure each course of bricks is level, that the sides of the wall are vertical (plumb) and that any corners are square. Fit a string line between the corners or ends, using corner blocks or pins inserted into the lowest mortar course, as a guide for laying the rest of the first course.

2 Lay the first whole course of bricks between the corners (or ends), following the string line. The last (closure) brick will need to be 'buttered' at both ends to form the vertical cross mortar joints on either side of it.

3 Continue laying whole courses, keeping the mortar joints to a consistent 10 mm thickness and checking all the time for level and plumb. Move the string line up as you go and build up the corners so

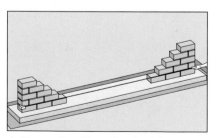

1 Use string lines fixed with pins or corner blocks to check that the courses are level and aligned.

3 When building up a corner, use a straight piece of timber to check the alignment of the courses.

that they are always higher than the rest of the brickwork. To check the alignment of the corners, use a straight piece of timber held against the wall. Tap any outstanding bricks back into place.

4 Shaped mortar joints must be finished while the mortar is wet. For weatherstruck joints and round iron jointing this is normally done after laying every second course; rake joints and V-joints are usually finished every four or six courses.

STEPPING UP

If you need to step up the brickwork, always use two level string lines. The top line runs right across the stepped gap, from the end of the built-up wall to a course above the step (see the drawing opposite). The second line is used on the lowest course so that the brickwork runs into the step evenly.

WALL JUNCTIONS

Where two walls meet in an L-junction, the brickwork of one wall must be tied in with that of the other. The tie-in ('toothing') bricks must extend into the other wall by at least one brick width.

If it is not possible to build both walls at once, holes known as 'indents' must be left in the first wall to take the tie-in bricks of the second when it is built later.

DAMP-PROOFING

Unlike house walls, which need a damp-proof course (DPC) built in to prevent damp from rising, garden walls do not need any special type of

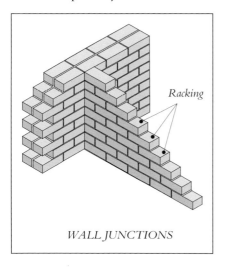

Racking

WALL JUNCTIONS

Indent

Block indent

INDENTS

Saddle-back brick units used to provide an overlapping coping to shed rainwater. A matching coping has been used to finish the piers.

damp-proofing. Where walls are in contact with damp soil (retaining walls, or garden wall courses below ground, for example) special or engineering bricks must be used and retaining walls need to have some drainage built in to them to prevent water build-up behind the wall (see page 38 for details).

What all walls need, however, is some kind of finishing at the top to prevent vertical penetration of the brickwork (which could lead to frost damage) and to throw rainwater away from the face of the wall.

The simplest method of finishing a wall is to lay bricks on edge or on end at the top of the wall (a 'soldier' course); equally simple is to add a course of shaped coping bricks or overlapping coping stones (common on reconstituted stone walls).

The traditional way of finishing off a brick wall is to use a soldier course, sandwiching a 'creasing' layer of protruding clay tiles.

Brick-on-edge soldier course capping plus tile creasing.

CURVED WALLS

SETTING OUT A CIRCLE

For a complete circle, fix a stake in the centre and tie a piece of string the radius of the circle to it. Attach a metal stake to the other end and use to draw the circle, keeping the string taut all the time. Determine the width of the foundation trench, adjust the length of the string and draw circles for either side of the trench. Curved walls can be set out in the same way but you may need to use a hose pipe to mark the outline of the curve.

CHOOSING BRICKS

Curved walls are most easily laid in header bond. For curves of a small radius, bricks can be cut to a tapered shape. Normal bricks may be used for curved walls and the mortar joints tapered, but only if the radius is more than 1 m or the joints will be too thick.

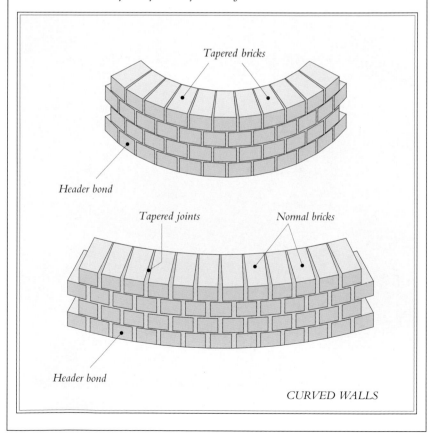

Tapered bricks

Header bond

Tapered joints   Normal bricks

Header bond

CURVED WALLS

A typical double-thickness garden wall, built in Flemish bond with intermediate piers. The wall and the piers have been finished with brick-on-edge capping and two courses of tile creasing.

Brick walls

Brick walls take many forms but the bricklaying requirements are much the same. Low garden walls are suitable projects for a home builder, as long as a few basic rules are followed.

TYPES OF BRICK WALL

There are many different types of brick wall an amateur might consider building around the home and the garden.

• Dividing walls are the most common, to form visual breaks between patio and lawn, for example, or to define the edges of pathways. Often low, dividing walls are usually a single brick thickness.

• Boundary walls surround the garden and provide both privacy and security. Normally double thickness, a boundary wall can be built up to 1.8 m (6 ft) high. For walls higher than 2 m (6 ft 6 in), local council permission and professional structural advice will be needed.

• Retaining walls are used to create terraces in sloping gardens and also to hold back raised flowerbeds. See page 36 for more details.

• Brick and block walls are used for many garden features such as a barbecues (see page 44) or planters (see page 42). Some can be treated like dividing walls, others like retaining walls.

• Screen walls neatly divide off a section of the garden without completely obscuring what is behind. They are built with pierced screen

TOOLS AND MATERIALS

See boxes on pages 10, 14, 20 and 24.

• Facing bricks

• Metal wall ties

• Expansion joint filler

walling blocks and pilaster piers—see pages 48–51 for further details.

DESIGNING A BRICK WALL

The way a brick wall is built depends on its height and purpose—retaining walls, in particular, need careful design (see page 36).

A single-thickness brick wall up to 450 mm (18 in) high is well within the capabilities of an amateur. It may not even need a concrete foundation (if there is a solid paved area to build on) and does not need supporting piers.

All other walls will need a proper foundation as described on page 13. Single thickness walls up to 675 mm (2 ft 3 in) and double thickness walls higher than 1.35 m (4 ft 6 in) will need supporting piers at the ends and at intervals of 3 m for long walls.

Piers should be twice the thickness of the wall and can be centred on the wall or project to one side. They should be bonded to the

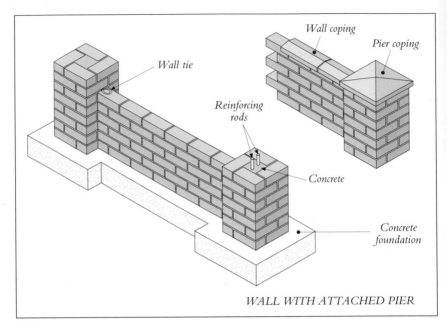

WALL WITH ATTACHED PIER

brickwork of the wall or secured to it using wall ties in each mortar course. A hollow pier will be stronger if you fill the void with concrete containing metal reinforcing rods anchored in the foundations. Remember to allow enough extra bricks to build the piers.

CAPPINGS AND COPINGS

Use a capping or coping on top of the wall to stop rainwater penetrating the brickwork. Brick cappings are the most convenient and they can be laid on edge or as a header course.

DAMP-PROOFING

A damp-proof course weakens the structure of a garden wall. Use special quality or engineering bricks for the courses below ground level. This will give adequate protection.

EXPANSION JOINTS

In long walls, include open expansion joints at a maximum of 12 m apart (usually where a panel meets a pier) to prevent cracking. Fill the gap with expansion joint filler.

FOOTINGS

Use foundation mix concrete to provide structural strength. The

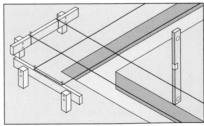

1 Set out the site with timber profiles and string lines and dig the foundation trenches.

recommended width of a concrete footing (foundation) is usually twice the width of the brick wall; the depth of the footing will depend on the height of the wall, the weight it is going to carry and the type of soil. See page 13 for further information on footings.

BUILDING A BRICK WALL

1 Calculate the number of bricks required (see the box on page 9). Set out the site with timber profiles and string lines to indicate the outlines of footing and wall. Allow for piers if necessary. Check the lines for level and dig foundation trenches (see pages 10–13).

2 Mix and pour the concrete footings, inserting reinforcement if required (see pages 14–18).

3 Move string lines to the width of the brickwork; check for level. Set out the first course dry to check the bonding and establish the corners, or use a gauging stick. Work out the bonding for any piers.

4 Lay the bricks (see pages 24–30). Build up the corners first, using water-resistant bricks for the first three courses (certainly for all courses below ground level). Check the courses are vertical with a spirit level.

5 Complete the bricklaying, checking for level and plumb with a spirit level—using a timber straight-edge to check brick alignment.

6 Add capping or coping to stop water penetration. Clean excess mortar from the bricks (see page 40).

Black expansion joint filler has been used on this wall.

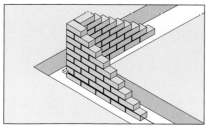

4 Build up the corners first, using water-resistant bricks for the first three courses.

5 Complete the bricklaying, checking for level and plumb (vertical). Check alignment with a batten.

Retaining walls

Retaining walls can be used for many different purposes: to make terraces on a sloping site or just to hold the soil in a garden bed. Small ones can be constructed by the home builder but high ones (1.2 m and over) should be designed by a structural engineer.

PLANNING

When planning a strong retaining wall you need to consider a number of factors:

● how much weight is to be retained by the wall;

● the materials that will be used for building the wall;

● what sort of drainage is required.

LOAD BEHIND THE WALL

The soil load behind a retaining wall puts great pressure on it, which is why a high retaining wall should always be designed by a structural engineer or it may collapse after heavy rain. Never use clay soil for backfilling as it expands and shrinks, and the wall may crack. Use hardcore topped with sandy soil.

RETAINING WALL MATERIALS

You can use any of the normal wall building materials for creating a retaining wall.

Bricks (or reconstituted stone blocks) are the usual choice, but bricks must be water-resistant and should be laid either as a full brick thickness wall, preferably with one of the stronger bonds (English bond or Flemish bond), or as two single skins (a bit like a cavity wall) held together with wall ties, with the gap between filled with concrete or mortar and reinforced with vertical steel bars. Retaining walls more than 1 m (3 ft 3 in) high need to be reinforced with piers at least at either end. High walls may need to have three thickness of brick for the first few courses.

Hollow concrete blocks are another good choice as you can fill the voids with concrete (and reinforcing bars)—but you will want to paint the exposed surface or to cover it with some kind of render.

Natural stone is also a good choice for a retaining wall (since it is heavy), but the wall will need to be much thicker at the bottom and laid to a 'batter'—that is, leaning slightly backwards into the slope.

All retaining walls should be built with full concrete foundations and a 'strong' mortar mix should always be used (see page 21).

A steep slope has been terraced and a series of retaining walls built to support wide garden beds. The high wall was professionally designed to withstand the pressure of the soil and rainwater behind it.

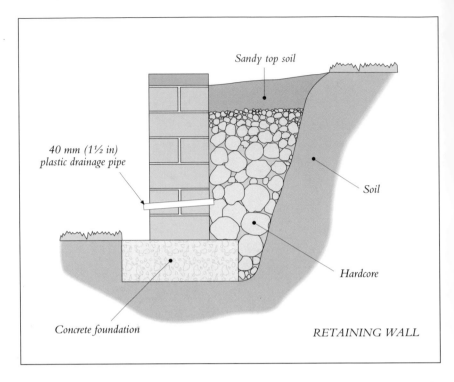

Sandy top soil

40 mm (1½ in)
plastic drainage pipe

Soil

Hardcore

Concrete foundation

RETAINING WALL

DRAINAGE

Water will collect behind a retaining wall and you must provide some way for it to be removed. The simplest method is to leave 'weep' holes by not putting mortar in some of the vertical joints low down in the wall; alternatively, you can install 40 mm plastic drainage pipes passing through the wall from the backfilling material.

If a large amount of water comes through the wall, you may need to install a surface drain on the ground below the wall to take it away.

ATTACHED PIERS

If a very strong wall is required, add attached piers (usually one and a half or two bricks square) at the back. Filled with concrete or mortar, they are reinforced with vertical steel bars.

BUILDING A RETAINING WALL

1 Calculate the number of bricks required (see page 9) allowing for piers. Remove enough soil from the site to lay the foundations and to build the wall—if necessary, hold the soil back with heavy timber boards. Set out timber profiles for the footing and wall positions, including piers, and excavate the trench for the footings (see pages 10–13).

2 Place steel reinforcement in the trench if required and pour in the

concrete. A retaining wall should be centred on its concrete footings. Anchor bars vertically for the piers and ensure the top of the footings is level (see pages 14–18).

3 Lay the bricks (see pages 24–30), leaving weep holes every third vertical (cross) joint in the first full course of bricks above ground level or installing regular drainage pipes through the wall, chipping the corners off bricks as necessary to fit.

4 Backfill behind the wall with hardcore (stones and broken bricks), with the largest pieces at the bottom, and finish off with light sandy soil.

5 Clean the brickwork (see page 40).

Retaining walls have been used here to hold back the garden and to create a patio area with raised flowerbeds.

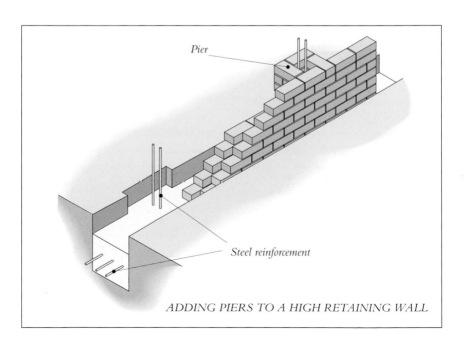

Pier

Steel reinforcement

ADDING PIERS TO A HIGH RETAINING WALL

Curved walls

A curved wall makes a stylish garden feature whether it is freestanding or used for a small structure such as the raised planter shown opposite.

TOOLS AND MATERIALS

See boxes on pages 10, 14, 20 and 24.

CIRCULAR PLANTER

1 Choose the bricks and assemble your materials and tools. Facing bricks are suitable for a planter as they do not absorb water. Use a strong mortar mix of one part cement, one quarter part lime and four parts sand (1:^{1}/$_4$:4).

2 Lay out the circular shape (see the box on page 31). Dig out the trench.

3 Lay the concrete foundations (see pages 14–18). Steel reinforcement is not necessary for a low wall. In fact, if the wall is only a few courses high, a 50 mm layer of sand or existing paving may be sufficient foundation.

4 Set out the entire first course of bricks, allowing for the tapered joints, and adjust the joints as necessary. Circular shapes are best laid entirely in header bond.

5 Lay the bricks (see pages 24–30), checking for level and plumb. Add a capping to stop water penetration.

6 Clean the bricks (see below).

CLEANING BRICKS
Let the brickwork dry for three days and clean off all excess mortar. Bricks are best cleaned with a solution of hydrochloric acid and water, one part acid to twenty parts water. Always add the acid to the water so the acid will be less likely to splash you.

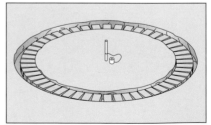

2 Set out the circular shape using a string from a central stake, then dig out the foundation trench.

4 Set out the entire first course, allowing for the tapered joints, and adjust the joints as necessary.

Curved walls are best laid in header bond, and in this large planter the top course was laid on edge to produce a neat capping course. Facing bricks were used for the project and the joints tapered to produce the curve.

Concrete walling blocks

Reconstituted stone concrete walling blocks make a change from clay bricks. They introduce an additional range of pleasing effects and can sometimes be easier to lay.

PLANNING

Concrete walling blocks come in a range of styles and finishes, many to imitate genuine stone walling. Some are brick-sized; others are larger. Blocks have one, two or three finished faces and also come in two-thirds lengths (to avoid cutting). Most ranges of concrete walling have their own matching capping in sizes to suit the main walling.

Concrete blocks can be laid in mortar (1:1:5 for Portland cement: lime:sand or 1:4 for masonry cement: sand) in exactly the same way as bricks—the alternative with some types of concrete block is to use walling adhesive which you apply with a spreader.

BUILDING A CONCRETE BLOCK WALL

A concrete block wall is set out in exactly the same way as a brick wall. High or thick walls will need proper concrete foundations (see page 13), but low single-thickness walls can be built on a compacted bed of sand or on existing paving (a paving slab patio, for example).

Check the manufacturer's literature for the number of blocks required for each square metre of walling—note the adhesive gives only a 3 mm gap between blocks. If foundations are required, set out the

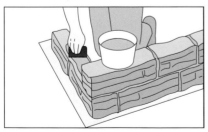

Walling adhesive is applied to the foundations or on the blocks already laid with a spreader.

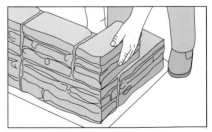

Large concrete walling blocks make laying quicker. This two-thirds block is being used to finish a corner.

site with timber profiles and string lines and dig out trenches before mixing and pouring the concrete for the foundations (see pages 10–18).

With mortar, set out and lay the blocks as for bricks (pages 24–30). Alternatively, spread a layer of walling adhesive on the foundation or the blocks already laid. Complete the blocklaying, checking for level and plumb (large blocks make laying quicker). Add matching capping stones, using more mortar or walling adhesive. Leave to set.

Reconstituted stone blocks, complete with their own capping, have been used for the retaining wall holding the flowerbed and the rear boundary wall.

Barbecue

A brick or concrete block barbecue is an excellent beginner's project and makes an attractive and useful addition to the garden. Add provision for fuel storage and surfaces for serving food.

PLANNING

When planning a barbecue, you need to consider the following.

- Size—how many people will it have to cook for?
- The fuel to be used—charcoal in a tray is the normal choice, but you should be able to adapt this design to suit a bottled gas barbecue.
- The location—choose a level site, sheltered from the wind, with access to the kitchen. Avoid fire hazards such as overhanging branches and timber fencing and think about the effects on your neighbours.

FOUNDATIONS

A barbecue is a light structure and, except on very soft soil, a 50 mm layer of compacted sand or existing paving such as a patio should be sufficient.

If you do lay foundations, use a foundation mix concrete (see pages 14–18 for details).

MATERIALS

A barbecue can be built from well-burnt bricks (not calcium silicate) which will be able to withstand the heat from the barbecue.

This project uses concrete walling blocks, which come in two sizes (standard and two-thirds lengths). The normal blocks have just one finished face; 'quoin end' blocks have a finished end as well and are used for exposed ends and corners; all other faces are flat and smooth.

A barbecue 'kit' consists of a cooking grill and a tray for holding the charcoal and it can be secured to the walls with wallbolts held in holes drilled into the walls or inserted in the mortar courses.

A storage area is incorporated under the charcoal tray and the top of the barbecue is finished off with coping stones. A paving slab provides a seat or serving area.

If mortar is used for constructing the barbecue it should be a fairly weak mix (1:1:6 cement:lime:sand) which will allow a little movement as the blocks heat up and cool down.

A patio next to the house is an ideal site for building a permanent brick or block barbecue. The patio paving will provide sufficient foundation.

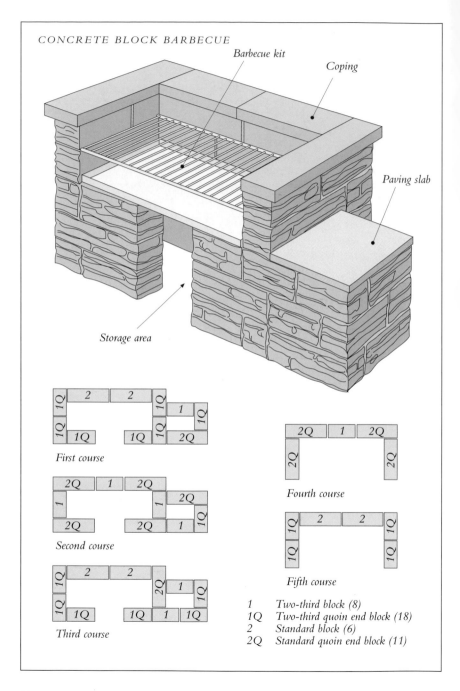

CONCRETE BLOCK BARBECUE

Barbecue kit

Coping

Paving slab

Storage area

First course

Second course

Third course

Fourth course

Fifth course

1	Two-third block (8)
1Q	Two-third quoin end block (18)
2	Standard block (6)
2Q	Standard quoin end block (11)

BUILDING THE BARBECUE

1 You do not need to lay concrete foundations for a simple barbecue. Existing paving should be perfectly satisfactory or use a 50 mm layer of well-compacted sand. Make sure, however, that the surface is level.

2 Lay the blocks dry on the surface, fitted around the barbecue kit. Mark the surface for the first course, taking the marked lines beyond the blocks, and spread a bed of mortar or a layer of walling adhesive.

3 Starting at one corner, lay a 'quoin end' block, adjusting it until it is aligned with the marks, and then lay the next block up against it, with more mortar or adhesive in between.

4 Continue building up three courses, using more mortar or adhesive, following the diagrams opposite. Use a spirit level to ensure that each course is horizontal and that the walls are vertical.

5 Once the fourth and fifth courses have been built on the main structure the basic barbecue is complete. If using mortar, the supporting bolts for the charcoal tray and cooking grill can be built into the mortar joints below the fourth and fifth courses.

6 Lay the single 450 mm square paving slab on the hollow seat (again using mortar or adhesive—unless you want it to be removable for an additional storage area) and fit the copings to the top of the fifth course of blocks. The coping blocks will need to be cut down to size to allow a 12 mm ($1/2$ in) overhang for the side pieces and to fit the two pieces at the back. Cut them by first making a groove around the cutting line with a club hammer and cold chisel and then giving the line a gentle tap with the same tools.

7 If you have used adhesive, drill holes in the walls to fit the wallbolts —two at each side for the cooking grill and two at the back for the charcoal tray (which sits on blocks at the front). Put in the bolts, using a spanner, and put the grill and charcoal tray in place.

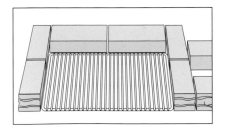

2 Lay the first course of blocks out dry around the barbecue kit to make sure they are correctly positioned.

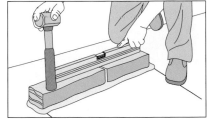

3 Start at a corner laying a quoin end block to the marked lines. Lay the next block and check levels.

Screen block walling

A screen block wall can be used in lots of different ways in the garden—and has the advantage that it will allow both light and air to pass through it. It is easy to build.

TOOLS AND MATERIALS

See boxes on pages 10, 14, 20 and 24.
- Pierced screen blocks
- Pilaster blocks
- Coping for walls and piers
- Metal reinforcing rods
- Wire mesh reinforcing
- Walling adhesive and spreader

USES

A screen block wall is normally used to divide one part of a garden from another where you do not want total exclusion. It is ideal around a patio to provide privacy and shelter without a significant loss of light and air. It can also be used effectively to 'hide' parts of the garden you do not want to be seen—a composting area, dustbins and so on.

MATERIALS

• Pierced screen blocks are made from concrete and usually coloured white or off white. They are 290 mm square and 90 mm thick and are about 50 per cent air, which allows light through (matching patterned solid blocks are also available). Screen blocks can be used on their own or incorporated in walling with reconstituted stone blocks.

• Unusually, for walling, pierced screen walling blocks are laid in stack bond (one on top of another); the wall is normally given strength by pilaster blocks, built as piers, which have a locating groove in one or more sides to support the screen blocks. Pilasters with one groove are used at the ends of walls; corner pilasters and intermediate pilasters (fitted every 3 m) have two grooves.

• Each pilaster block is 190 mm high, so three blocks (plus two 10 mm mortar courses) is equal to two screen blocks (plus one 10 mm mortar course). The pilasters are hollow, and can be filled with mortar and reinforced with steel rods set into the foundation concrete.

• Matching 600 mm copings are made for the walling blocks and decorative caps for the pilaster piers. Coping stones help to hold the wall together as well as protecting it and improving its appearance.

• Screen block walling can be built using mortar as for brick walls (except that you should use white Portland cement and sand), but you can also use walling adhesive—more appropriate when using them with reconstituted stone walling blocks.

Pierced screen blocks often make effective dividing or boundary walls. They allow air and light through so are good for plants.

PLANNING

Low screen block walls (up to 1 m) can be built directly on existing paving, but walls higher than this will need a proper concrete foundation as for brick walls.

Additional strength is provided by reinforcing rods inside the pilasters and also by wire mesh laid where the wall bed joints coincide with the pilaster bed joints.

When planning the length and height of the wall, remember that you must work in units of 300 mm—and it will be better with lengths in multiples of 600 mm, so that you do not have to cut coping stones to fit.

BUILDING A SCREEN BLOCK WALL

1 Calculate the number of blocks required—eleven for each square metre of walling, but remember that the wall must be designed in units of 300 mm or, preferably, 600 mm.

2 Set out the site with timber profiles and string lines to indicate the outlines of the footings and the wall and the position of the pilaster piers. Check the lines for level and dig trenches (see pages 10–13).

3 Mix and pour the concrete footings (see pages 14–18), inserting steel reinforcement starter bars at the positions of the pilaster piers. Extend these bars once the concrete has set by wiring on reinforcing rods.

4 Move the string lines to the width of the pilaster piers and set pilaster and walling blocks out dry (with spacers to simulate the 10 mm mortar gaps) to check the spacing. The piers should not be more than 3 m (ten blocks) apart.

5 Mortar the first pilaster pier in place around a starter bar and reinforcing rod (see pages 24–30 for trowelling techniques), taking it up two blocks. Position the first two blocks of the second pier without mortar and set a string line over the top of the two piers to act as a guide when laying the walling blocks.

6 Spread mortar on the foundations

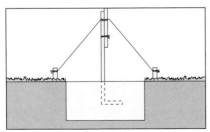

3 When laying the foundations, incorporate an L-shaped steel starter bar for the pier reinforcing rods.

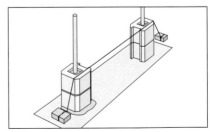

5 With the first two pilaster blocks mortared into place, set up the other pier dry and lay a string line.

sufficient for two blocks. Dampen the blocks with water first (to prevent the mortar drying out too quickly) and lay them on the mortar bed, buttering one side of each block with mortar. The first block must be fitted firmly into the locating groove in the pilaster pier. Continue laying the first course of blocks, using a spirit level to make sure it is level.

7 When you get to the position of the second pier, mortar the first block of this in place as well—and continue the first course to further piers if the wall is longer than 3 m or goes round a corner. Then lay the second course of walling blocks (this time slotting both end blocks into their piers).

8 After the second course of walling blocks, add the third pilaster block (which should be level) and lay some metal reinforcing mesh in the next mortar bed over the top of the walling blocks taking it into the pier. Add another pilaster block and fill the centre of the pilaster piers with mortar. Continue laying pilaster

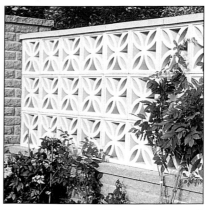

Screen block walling (here used without pilasters) can be very effectively incorporated into a reconstituted stone block wall.

blocks and screen walling blocks until the wall is the finished height, using more mesh reinforcing strip every other walling course.

9 Finish off by adding the coping stones on top of the walling blocks, mortaring these in place, and adding caps to the pilaster piers. Clean all loose mortar off the face of the walling blocks and pilaster piers and give the mortar in the joints a neat recessed or flush finish.

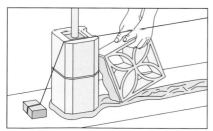

6 The first screen block needs to be buttered with mortar on one side and is inserted into the pilaster groove.

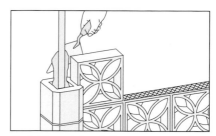

8 Add metal reinforcement mesh to every other screen mortar course and fill the pilaster piers with mortar.

Paving basics

Bricks, concrete blocks and clay pavers are ideally suited to paving, as they are decorative while being durable and resistant to abrasion. They can be used for paths or larger areas such as patios.

TOOLS AND MATERIALS

- Bricks, blocks or clay pavers
- Bedding material (coarse to medium sand, hardcore or mortar)
- String line and pegs
- Spirit level
- Tape measure
- Two timber screeding rails (40 x 40 mm and 6 m long)
- Screed stick (piece of straight timber)
- Compacting equipment (tamper, hired compactor or rubber mallet)

ADVANTAGES

Bricks, concrete blocks or clay pavers are much more pleasing to look at than solid concrete or asphalt. They come in a wide range of colours and can be laid in a variety of patterns.

Bricks, blocks and pavers can be laid quickly and the area used immediately. They are durable and hard-wearing (except for old, soft bricks, which should not be used), and the hard, smooth surface makes them easy to clean.

Minor surface cracks in the joints and gentle undulations in brick and block paving are inconspicuous. Repairs can be made easily as individual bricks can be removed and, provided a good match is achieved for the existing material, the repair will be virtually invisible.

PLANNING

Paving must be able to withstand everyday use, the occasional heavy load and stresses caused by tree roots. Consider, too, whether you will need to gain access to underground services (gas, water, electricity and drains) from time to time.

BASE COURSE

Take time to prepare the site properly as your brickwork will only be as good as the foundations. The base course will depend on the type of paving that is being laid and how you are going to use the paving.

For a path or patio you may need only 50 mm of sand as a base, but for a surface that has to take heavy loads, 100 mm of hardcore topped with 50 mm of sand is recommended. To achieve maximum strength the base material should be well compacted.

For a more solid base you can use a 50 mm deep mortar bedding which has the added advantage that it won't be washed away by rain water. The mortar mix should be one part cement to four parts clean, washed sharp sand.

Old bricks were used for this path. The sweeping patterns of the paving are reflected in the curved walls that retain the garden beds.

CALCULATING QUANTITIES

For normal-sized bricks (see page 5) laid on sand, allow 46 bricks for each square metre, plus 5 per cent allowance for cutting and breakage.

For bricks laid in mortar (with a 10 mm joint between them), allow 40 bricks for each square metre; clay pavers are generally the same length and width as bricks, but are thinner. Concrete blocks are smaller (200 x 100 mm) and you will need 50 bricks for each square metre plus 5 per cent for wastage.

Sand is sold by the cubic metre or by the tonne (1 cubic metre = 1.5 tonnes) and for a 50 mm thickness you will need 0.5 cubic metre for 10 square metres of paving. You will need twice the volume of hardcore if this is required, but you may already have suitable stones around the site.

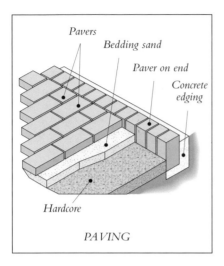

Pavers

Bedding sand

Paver on end

Concrete edging

Hardcore

PAVING

BRICK PATTERNS

Bricks can be laid either straight or at 45 degree angles, and in a wide variety of patterns (see the diagrams below). The most popular patterns are running (stretcher), herringbone and basketweave. Basic patterns can also be combined to make more elaborate designs, for example, combined running and stack bond.

Plan the paving carefully to avoid cutting bricks, blocks or pavers— though cutting will be inevitable if you use a diagonal pattern. Paving may have to be positioned to work around an obstacle such as a tree.

Work carefully when laying the patterns. Use string lines to keep the bricks in a straight line and use a straight-edge to keep them level and straight. If you are paving a large area, divide it into smaller sections with string lines so that the pattern remains tight (see the diagram below right). Start from the lowest point and work towards the top.

DRAINAGE

Paved areas must be adequately drained, by giving the paving a slope of 1 in 60 to allow water to run off (preferably away from the house).

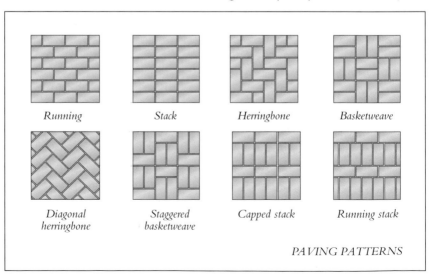

Running

Stack

Herringbone

Basketweave

Diagonal herringbone

Staggered basketweave

Capped stack

Running stack

PAVING PATTERNS

EDGINGS

Use edge restraints to prevent the bricks and base material moving and to stop the bricks around the edges of the area sinking. When setting out the edges, take into consideration the size of the bricks and joints. This way you won't have to cut bricks to fit. The edging can be timber, solid concrete bricks or a proprietary concrete edging.

• For a timber edging use durable timber or treated pine that is straight and free of knots and splits. Fix it in place with stakes. Use scarf joints to join timbers as they are less obvious. Place gravel under the timber to help drainage and reduce rotting.

• A solid concrete edging can be made separately or as part of a concrete base. Use foundation concrete mix ($1:2^1/_2:3^1/_2$, cement: sand:aggregate) with formwork to hold it while it sets.

• A brick edging (bricks-on-edge or bricks in a sawtooth pattern) should be laid on a mortar bed, preferable on a concrete foundation.

• Proprietary edgings in various styles are made by concrete block manufacturers and are set in mortar.

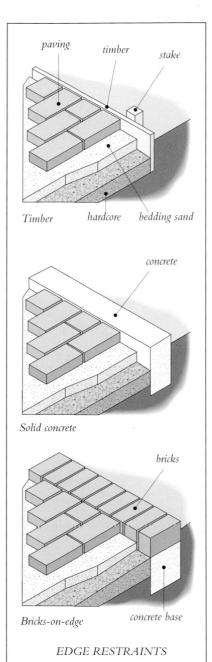

paving *timber* *stake*

Timber *hardcore* *bedding sand*

concrete

Solid concrete

bricks

Bricks-on-edge *concrete base*

EDGE RESTRAINTS

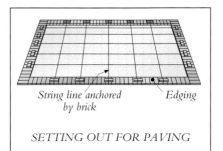

String line anchored by brick *Edging*

SETTING OUT FOR PAVING

Path with sand base

Bricks, blocks or clay pavers can be used to make an attractive and hard-wearing path. Laying a brick path on a sand base requires little specialist skill, just care and attention to detail.

METHOD

Planning a path is the same as other paving. See pages 52–5 for details.

1 Work out the brick pattern you want to use. A path should be at least 1.2 to 1.5 m wide to allow two people to pass on it, but work out the precise width to fit the sizes of the bricks, blocks or pavers you are using. Lay out the path, setting up string lines and maintaining an even width. Curved paths can be laid out using a hose pipe as a guide. The surface should have a slight slope to shed water.

2 Excavate the area to the required depth (50 mm for the sand plus the depth of the brick, block or paver). Place the bedding sand in and spread it evenly over the area to a depth of about 55 mm and compact it lightly with a tamper—a length of timber with a square, flat base.

3 Set the timber screeding rails into the sand with their tops at the required height and then level off the sand with a screed stick. Fill any hollows and low areas with sand.

4 If using brick or concrete edgings, lay them now, or fix timber edgings in place. Allow concrete or mortar to set before proceeding.

5 Lay the bricks, starting from the lowest point of the path and working up. Butt the bricks firmly against one another and use a straight-edge on each line of bricks to keep them level. Use a spirit level to check for a consistent level or slope.

2 Spread the bedding sand over the area and compact it with a tamping timber with a square, flat base.

3 Set your screeding rails at the required height and then level off the sand with a screed stick.

Laid in stretcher bond with headers for the edges, this path of clay pavers was simple to lay. The slightly winding route (laid out first with a hose pipe) adds interest to a narrow garden.

6 When the paving and edge restraints are secure, sweep fine sand over the whole area until the joints are completely filled.

7 Compact the brick pavers to the correct level, using either a rubber mallet or a heavy hammer and scrap timber to spread the impact. Remove excess sand from the surface.

7 Compact the brick pavers to the correct level, using either a rubber mallet or hammer plus timber.

Patio

A patio can be built successfully with a sand base but for areas of heavy 'traffic' a firm base may be needed. Hardcore and sand are customary; a mortar base would also be suitable.

METHOD
See pages 52–5 for general paving planning; then follow these steps.

1 Decide on your paver pattern and edging type and determine the precise size of the patio accordingly so that the pavers fit neatly. Lay out the area using string lines and prepare the area for the base.

2 Excavate the area to the required depth (150 mm plus the depth of the pavers). Place the hardcore in it and compact it so it is 100 mm deep, using a hired plate compactor or a roller. Add bedding sand and spread it evenly over the area to a depth of 55 mm (allowing for compaction).

3 Add the edge restraints and fit intermediate screeding rails.

4 Level off the sand with a screed stick, which can be notched to the required depth so it fits over the edgings. Fill any hollows and low areas with sand.

5 Lay the pavers, starting from the lowest point and working up. Each paver must be butted firmly against its neighbours and each line of pavers should then be tested with a straight-edge to ensure that it is level and straight.

6 When the paving has all been laid, sweep sand over the whole area until the joints are completely filled.

7 Compact the pavers to the correct level using a hired plate vibrator, placed on a piece of plywood to stop the pavers being chipped.

2 Lay out the area to fit the chosen brick pattern and then excavate it to the required depth.

4 Level off the sand with a screed stick and then fill hollows and low areas with sand.

Clay brick pavers laid in a herringbone pattern make an interesting surface for a patio or courtyard. They are hard wearing and easy on the eye.

5 Lay the pavers, starting from the lowest point and working your way up. Keep to the pattern.

7 Compact the pavers to the correct level using a compactor placed on ply to stop the bricks being chipped.

Bricking up openings

Bricking up an unwanted opening—a doorway or window—is a fiddly job and to get a good result you need to lay the bricks correctly and match the materials.

METHOD

1 Select bricks and mortar to match the existing ones (see box on page 9). Match bricks for colour, texture and size. Remove the timber frames and wedges from the openings, taking care not to damage the brickwork.

2 Remove any half bricks from the edges of the opening so that the bonding will continue unbroken. Clean all mortar from the brickwork in the opening. Work slowly so as not to damage brick corners or crack the bricks. Hard mortar joints may need to be drilled out or cleaned out with a plugging chisel.

3 Set out the first course to make sure the new courses will align exactly with the old ones. You may need to cut the bricks for the first course so that they will fit properly and allow the upper courses to align.

4 Thoroughly wet the old brickwork so the new mortar will bond to it with maximum strength.

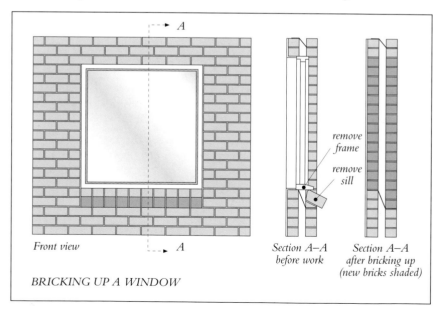

Front view

    A

BRICKING UP A WINDOW

remove frame

remove sill

Section A–A before work

Section A–A after bricking up (new bricks shaded)

5 Lay the bricks, using a string line or straight-edge to keep each course level. Completely fill the bed joints and cross joints with mortar. Take care to keep the bricks level and plumb and aligned with the courses in the existing wall. Make a visual check after each course.

6 When laying the last course of bricks, add enough mortar to the top of the bricks to fill the joint completely so that the new brickwork is bonded as strongly as possible to the existing work.

7 Clean off all excess mortar from the bricks before they dry. The bricks can be cleaned with hydrochloric acid and water (20 parts water to 1 part acid) three days after you have finished the bricklaying.

The doorway above this stone threshold has been partly bricked up and a window inserted. A neater result could have been obtained by using cut bricks for the first course instead of bricks laid on edge. The bricks could not be matched exactly and so the wall has been painted.

Repairing brickwork

Crumbling mortar and broken bricks can be replaced, and cracks repaired, without damaging the rest of the wall.

REPOINTING AND REPLACING BRICKS

One of the most common problems of brick walls is crumbling mortar. If you see deteriorating joints, you can replace the mortar to prevent major faults developing. Broken bricks are removed and replaced the same way.

1 Use a plugging chisel and a club hammer to remove any mortar that is loose or around broken bricks. Remove the bed joint first, then the top joint and then the two cross joints. Remove the brick.

2 Clean the cavity. Use a paint brush to dampen the bricks to prevent the mortar drying out too quickly.

3 Mix up mortar to a suitable colour and consistency. Replace the mortar on the bed joint first, then the cross joints and then apply mortar to the top of the brick. Replace the brick slowly, making sure the mortar does not fall off. Ensure any gaps in the mortar are filled. You can support the brick on a piece of plywood as you slide it in.

4 Repoint the mortar, making sure that the joints have the same profile as the existing joints.

CRACKS

Cracks appear in brickwork when the structure settles or shifts. They should be repaired before they get too large by removing the mortar to a depth of at least 5 cm (2 in) or until the mortar is solid. Then replace the mortar as described above.

Cracks that reappear may indicate a serious problem. Consult a building surveyor to determine the cause.

1 Remove all mortar, removing the bed joint first, then the top joint, then the two cross joints.

3 Mortar the bed and cross joints and the top of the brick. Replace the brick and fill any gaps.

Tools for bricklaying

Some of the most useful tools for bricklaying are shown below. Build up your tool kit gradually—most of the tools can be purchased from your local hardware store.

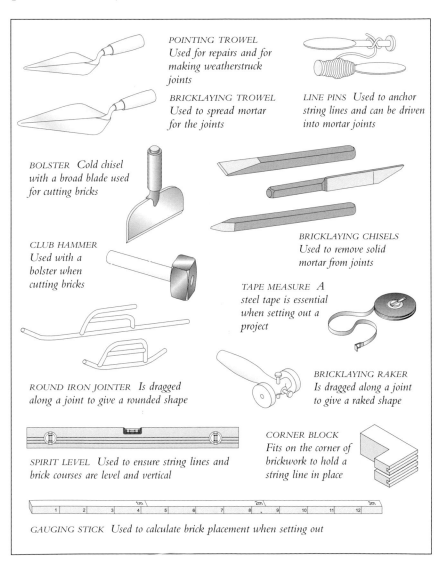

POINTING TROWEL *Used for repairs and for making weatherstruck joints*

BRICKLAYING TROWEL *Used to spread mortar for the joints*

LINE PINS *Used to anchor string lines and can be driven into mortar joints*

BOLSTER *Cold chisel with a broad blade used for cutting bricks*

CLUB HAMMER *Used with a bolster when cutting bricks*

BRICKLAYING CHISELS *Used to remove solid mortar from joints*

TAPE MEASURE *A steel tape is essential when setting out a project*

ROUND IRON JOINTER *Is dragged along a joint to give a rounded shape*

BRICKLAYING RAKER *Is dragged along a joint to give a raked shape*

SPIRIT LEVEL *Used to ensure string lines and brick courses are level and vertical*

CORNER BLOCK *Fits on the corner of brickwork to hold a string line in place*

GAUGING STICK *Used to calculate brick placement when setting out*

Index